# WAIT

*The Brittingham Prize in Poetry*

# WAIT

Alison Stine

The University of Wisconsin Press

The University of Wisconsin Press
1930 Monroe Street, 3rd Floor
Madison, Wisconsin 53711–2059
uwpress.wisc.edu

3 Henrietta Street
London WC2E 8LU, England
www.eurospanbookstore.com

5  4  3  2  1

Printed in the United States of America

Library of Congress Cataloging-in-Publication Data
Stine, Alison, 1978–
   Wait / Alison Stine.
      p.   cm. — (The Brittingham prize in poetry)
   ISBN 978-0-299-28314-8 (pbk.: alk. paper)
   ISBN 978-0-299-28313-1 (e-book)
   1. Teenage girls—Poetry.  I. Title.  II. Series: Brittingham prize in poetry
(Series)
   PS3569.T4834W35    2011
   811'.6—dc22
                                                    2010038897

*For Jordan*

# Contents

# Acknowledgments

I am grateful to the editors of the following magazines, where many of the poems in this book first appeared:

*Agni*: "Gossip"
*Barn Owl Review*: "Love Letter"
*Black Warrior Review*: "Hadrian's Wall" (as
    "To Draw a Line")
*Copper Nickel*: "Canary," "The Ladder Tree"
*Fourteen Hills*: "All the Animals Are Birds"
    (as "X All the Animals")
*Gulf Coast*: "Letter after Dismemberment"
*The Hat*: "Scissors, Hammer, Hoof Pick, Awl"
*Hayden's Ferry Review*: "Rabbit of the
    World"
*The Huffington Post*: "Phlox" (as "Odd
    Wild")
*The Kenyon Review*: "Stepmother," "Wife"
*Linebreak*: "Bug"
*No Tell Motel*: "Tennessee"
*Passages North*: "The Red Thread," "The
    Thief"
*Phoebe*: "Impetus," "White Asparagus"
*PN Review*: "The Land"
*Poetry*: "After the Party"
*Post Road*: "Salt"
*Prairie Schooner*: "The Flood"
*River City*: "Nothing Happened"
*Shenandoah*: "Velata"
*Valparaiso Poetry Review*: "Child Bride,"
    "Your Marriage" (as "Marriage")

"Clean" and "The Ripper's Bride" first appeared in the chapbook *Lot of My Sister* (The Kent State

University Press, 2001). Reprinted with permission of The Kent State University Press.

Thank you to Cornelius Eady, Ron Wallace, everyone at the University of Wisconsin Press, Ohio University, and the Denison University Reynolds Young Writers' Workshop. Special thanks to Dan Sweatt for the good luck, and to my friends, students, and family, especially my husband, Jordan Davis.

# WAIT

# Wife

We waited in the field like birds.
    We ran and hid in the fields to watch.

        Oh make me a big house. Make me

a blackbird. I want to be a blackbird.
    But I was not. I was hidden in beige.

        I was hard corn left for the animals.

We were hiding from men, our father
    and uncles, who would throw us

        in air, leave us in trees, mistake

for laughter our screams. On the back
    of their motorbikes, into our legs,

        the engines burned names.

One summer they killed the hornets
    by dosing the nest in gas, a turban

        in flames. The peacocks tore

at the cars. The hunting dogs
    were all chained. At the first dust

        swirl, I stood up. I got in a car

for a strawberry cream. Heat gave
    the road a ghost, and I wanted

        to be dancing. Now I want to be

a bird again. I want to be waiting.
  Why did we stop waiting? We were

    fine. We were fine, eating berry burrs

and mouse seed. The birds landed
  in our braided hair, and the men

    called but could not find us. You

were coming. You were coming.
  I didn't know. I would have curled

    in a rabbit whorl, a mouse nest,

in leaf-spilled shade. I am a bird
  in the field and I want you to find me.

    I want you to find me. Tell me *wait*.

*It's the devil I loved.*
Neko Case

I

# Child Bride

Women rise to the star loft. Women wait
at the back door, set platters before you,
bread and meat. Another woman washes.
It's different every night. Your sister
has two days before her wedding,
but she has been sewing since she was five.
Your cousin is nineteen, but her groom
is sixty. You risk salvation by squeezing
your eyes. Now your prophet is wheat
in a rain field. Now your prophet is acid
and orange. Love ends in the pocket, a rope
belt untying. The threads fissure like hair
in the hand. *What is your name and who
is your mother?* The halls are full of girls.
You get used to fingers. The boys are lost—leave
them. Leave behind your nineteen mothers.
Your father will never remember your name.

# Tennessee

It was easy to say young. It was easy to say

   summer. *Summer.* Fruit bled from trees.
      I loved a married man, and in the months

after, it was easy to say I wanted trust. I wanted

   wisdom. I wanted a father. Doctors said it,
      perched on chairs; friends, leaning over coffee.

But what I wanted was dead. What I wanted

   crawled into a Tennessee cave to die—
      the country singer, clad in black, hopped up

on amphetamines—but did not die, not then.

   The rocks were a balm, a choir of elbows.
      Jesus smiled from the water-cupped pit.

And when he returned, leaves clung to him,

   chest and limb. He sweated out the drugs,
      married, lived to be seventy, sang *holy, holy.*

It is not the going under. That we managed,

   ascending the stairs. Each push broke through
      my body until he was past my body, until

he was piercing the quilt, the frame, the rug,

   the floor, the plaster-stitched ceiling with perfect
      stars, a path like the newspaper picture

of the burned house: upstairs, a fire had cut

      through blankets and bed, clear to the first story
        in the sleeping shape of the child

who had died. He could give me death, enough

      skin to drown. What he could not give, what I
      wanted: it was to rise up.

# The Flood

The fava drowned and then the tomatoes.
Each rose in the lap of our blessing;
after so much drought, our answer:
the rain changing the earth like a chemical
boom. Solid be liquid, liquid be ever.
*That be a dollar*, said the Amish at market
when we lingered over their bread,
said as if willing the loaf's transformation
into our arms. So at first the rain
was welcome. We thought it was our doing.
Standing outside, the earth seemed
to open, gathering mud in pockets
like mouths. We did not see these were also
like lesions, wounds that would never
repair. Our seeds swam away in them.
Our shoes stuck at the bone.
In ditches and gullies, the grass ran
like cilia, and the water was not pure.
No. It was full of us, flaked with rock
and wood, the leavings of our bodies,
which left us, floated, were lost.

## The Thief

He took the pond, soured green.

    The green was from the woods.
    The rot was from the trees, the stumps

hauled up and planted like birds,

    the lady slippers and buttonbush,
    the chokecherry and ninebark.

He took dirt for the hill because the hill

    was thin, too thin to hold the feet
    of ferns. The moss had nested.

The vines all spread. The muskrat

    sprung a trap in shallow water.
    He took the rabbit's crown,

skunk's skull, fossilized deer from the deer

    graves. The shotgun warmed from its
    sleeping place. He took mold

from the mortar, and dammed the stream, damned

    my arms, damned my lips, damned
    my breasts. Goddamn my dress.

Let me have this: small hooked scar,

    the one above his forehead that fluttered
    into shape, the one his best friend

gave him, swinging for another guy.

Let me have this: time he told;
    our clothes, stepping stones

to the field where we lay before

    breaking, before bitterness, before
        discovery. Let me bring it to my mouth.

Let me pull it from my tongue, and candle

    to the light. And call it mine.

# Neighbor

I could imagine the lot, a yard;
    the apartment, a house with hyacinth

        I didn't plant but might have, basil

spiked with skunking hearts. Then:
    a cough. The woman upstairs on her own

        porch stirs, the gas-sharp fizz

as she strikes a match, lets it flutter.
    It goes out, soundless, falls to the ground,

        a blade among blades, missed at first.

The pictures were missed at first,
    swimming up to a television screen,

        the men's faces cut away, their bodies

blurred, careful as flowers.
    One could have been my lover's body,

        the way we turn, trying to break

out of our skin. But this man is bound
    in ropes, held by a soldier who wears

        my colors, colors of the country I used

to call home. Televisions used
    to go on and off with a pop, the gray

        explosion of a gathering dot. Later,

you could place your hand on top, and it
   would be warm. Darkness then picture—I know

      how it works. Once, my neighbor,

the morning after a party, threw a chest
   of ice and water over the rail. It came down

      hard. I jumped, having thought myself alone,

having let myself believe it. Looking up,
   I saw her porch, how much it sagged:

      the gray-gone boards, the insect holes,

the floor. How thin it was. How close.

# Gossip

Oh, it was good. I was good. *You're so good,*
he said. A purple miniskirt and a black
satin string. I smelled like cotton. I smoked
cigarettes with my legs. I sheared a windmill.
I ballpoint pen-etched our names. I was high
school. I was sweet breath, and when I caught
him in the laundry room, I pulled him down
in the lint. I had gum in my mouth and I
snapped it, and the gum reminded him
of a cat's crimp. I was a cat. I shaved. I was thin
as a breeze. It is true in the yard, in the barn,
by the flagpole. I had splinters in my shoulder,
and milk paint in my veins. My back was a yarn
scratch. I came. I came. Oh, you must have
been in a rabbit hole when I came. You must
have been a lawn mower blade. You were
the blood, the mosquito in the stump bath,
the black fly, the twig, the tick latching in the shade.
It is true in the middle of the day. It is true in the car
park, on the rooftop, the shingles thudding down
like rain. Everything you heard. Our bodies,
pale as stitched stars, made the shapes you say.
Strange how he never once mentioned, all
those times in the star bay, you: your stinking
mouth; your eyes, rat-black, blank and ablaze.

# Prize-Winning Photograph

Tired of party scenes—beads thickening
necks, the faces of the women glazed, so
forgetful—the newspaper photographer climbs.

Water slices from sky. There are men
on the ground, and through the bars
of the fire escape, he can see her dress, see

the revelers jostle to be first. Someone
is already calling for help. Or must be.
And what can he do but break the group

into frames, capture their want, the street
coined with rain, her breasts torn from cloth?
Nobody thinks to look up. Now he can hardly

breathe. Now the camera overheats, jams,
lens smoky. So it will be only ten shots—
and the one that wins, in which she rises,

belly bucking, fish skin. The paper censors
her face, as if a shadow fell there. She will
disappear, and so will the men, though they linger on

in parts, in pieces: legs driven among legs,
white teeth split open in grin. The hands
we know. They're ours.

# The Accident

You went away and wanted to do things,
  things that brought you to the edge

    of buildings, like this building

with its pool and its five stories.
  It was a hotel, it was not yours

    to jump from. Still, you jumped

from a balcony, thinking it was
  all right, you were all right.

    You were sailing in air, you were

going to make it, and you made it—
  almost—on an alcoholic cloud.

    One leg landed in a haze of blue,

the other on ground, which split
  you, then tipped you forward

    into water. Your friends, the ones

who had gone first, shook the spray
  from their eyes. They had bought

    the drinks, and bade you drink them,

found the stairs, and ascended.
  But what can be traced back to you?

    I hate people or else I love them,

like I love the little bones that were broken—
the finger, the wrist, each inch

a disobedience, splintered

as ice. Silver bubbles rose and spun.
Who fished you out, who dried

you off? Who was around

when you made up your mind?
I thought I knew the life I wanted,

the water rocking with waves

you made, that muffled boom
of the body. It was not there, then

it was there, upsetting everything.

# The Interpreter

It was something he was singing
like the ponds would sing if only
they would open their lovely mouths.
All day he taught strangers to open
their mouths, to enter the kingdom
of English. Teaching is love
of your own voice, and he is in love,
singing as the first men must have
when they realized what power,
the animal sounds. Bone makes a sound.
Skin makes a sound. The anvil ear
picks it up, and puts it out as information:
all the night noise amplified. What is it?
The whisk of the air-conditioner,
the brush of leg against leg? There are
not signs for everything, the interpreter
said when asked if she ever forgot words.
You make them up, get close enough.
Sign *insect* if you have forgotten *cicada*.
Later, you can go back, sign *seven year*,
sign *seeking heat*. Sign *burrowing*, sign *gone*.

## Velata

This is what you have missed, love:

    the Pearl has been named.
      It is a portrait from life.

It is a sitter who knew the painter

    behind muslin where he stood:
      Raphael, at the height of his fame.

He will be dead by thirty-seven,

    is engaged to a cardinal's niece,
      and every night shades ink pot

into eyelash, rose cup to breast,

    flesh of his wife—his real wife,
      a baker's daughter—the colors

bright as an egg's cracked plate.

    She is half-naked, half-glaze, sheer
      across her stomach, holding out

her breast. For you, I held

    my body barely in strings. For you,
      one shift and the white dress fell.

Now, at home, heat is a wire

    strung through cloth. I do these things
      you have asked of me. I keep you

hidden as a wound; every day

    of your absence, write a letter,
      sealed in my mouth for you.

Myrtle and quince, the secret

    gathers between them like a blister,
      capped with blood. Here is his

name on a blue sash banding

    her arm in two: flesh above, flesh
      below. Here is a bruise, butterfly

of your mouth, I bear for you.

    Is this what you wanted, the background
      burned, rushes, a well for her head?

Is this what men do, make

    mistresses from wives? His students hurry:
      *scrub the ring off, scrub the ring off,*

*scrub the ring off, scrub the ring—*

**II**

# The Bicycle

I practiced kissing on the ash
with its patch bare of bark
like a belly, and the knob
in the middle, a stunted arm
or tongue. At the backyard edge,
the grass fell away. I could see
how everything connected—
the earth to the white roots.
Into the trees, my family threw
objects in anger: a small rake; a glove,
fingers stuffed with leaves.
Branches grew around them.
I don't know if they knew. I swear
I remember a bicycle, back end
smashed, tire spinning errantly
in wind, as though still believing
it could run.

# Reelection

Everything is sharper. Birds become birds.

    Spearheads crystallize into trees. Those
        lines? They are called branches. That sky

with white? I had never seen. All the signs

    are signs we've forgotten. The wind makes
        mouths of them, yesterday's names.

And the love I left behind me turns to tip

    the shades. The television, left on all night,
        has told us dreams. Outside, the sky

is aluminum. The meat trucks strike a grate,

    and all the empty cages shake. They know;
        they miss their beating hearts. I have to

wait for them to cross the street, where yesterday

    a cow was killed. *I thought it was a deer*,
        the driver said. Waiting for the light

to bleed, for someone to notice I am in a man's

    pajama pants, borrowed stripes and gray.
        Only clothes will hold me to this world,

his clothes and the heart that was in them,

    the short hair, the heat, the shoulder wings.
        That time, after a fall, he held my hand

to count each bone? That is what I live for,

what I sought to save. *I thought it was
a deer*, the driver kept saying. *I thought*

*it was a bird, a kite, a tree.* Such things

are worth seeing. You have to bend yourself
back for them. You have to look until there is

no more looking, the wingspan lost to the leaves.

## The Flies

Only two blinder-eyed flies in the vestibule.

When I open the door, the flies go out,
sparks in a sky of grease-streaks,

car alarms. You go as you are called

to her arms, to mine. This is how you hold
a promise, hold your cells inside.

Your body drifts in mine, does not leave

a linger. When, the next day, there is a swirl
of flies, I watch through the inside door.

Hundreds hatch like dollars shot in air,

nothing given sudden shape, humming
their hope in the corners, tapping their legs

against glass. I cannot leave without leaving

a way in for them. Do you see now what I
wanted? Do you think of my body

winged? Fill me, as you promised. Find me

trapped, and let the hundreds go, let the little
ones outside. Bitter would not be bitter.

My petal tongue would rise. Cloud,

I drank you; you were mine. What of
the flies? Poison slunk beneath the gate;

I will give them halos. I will make them saints.

# All the Animals Are Birds

*A dog becomes a bird. A cow becomes a bird.*
   *A bird stays a bird.* The artist is explaining

      how he sees carousels, the animal

backs emerging from wood. He keeps
   finding himself returning to movement.

      The small gray bodies hop and stir.

They find their way into his hands,
   heads erupting like onions,

      bridges funneled to a beak,

the features stretched and grown.
   No one wants to ride a starling.

      They cannot run. They cannot beat

the tigers, the loam-nosed stallions
   children are drawn to, the ostriches,

      the ark—whichever neck pulls in front

as the music stops. Tonight I am struck
   with the secrecy of things. In my bath,

      the vitals pour. Shampoo syrups:

the scent is called sugar. The lip
   of the white tub is level with the window,

      and through it a boy in the backyard runs.

He is naked, feet tacked on the ends
　　of his legs so careless, so salt sprung.

　　In the yard there is little grass. This

is the first I have washed my body since
　　you tried to touch my body. The door

　　　　was light, the lock painted over. I watched

the bar in its silver cage. How the screws
　　want to open. How the wood wants to give.

　　　　Each cell, sprung free, is a step, is a bird,

is a bird *stays* a bird, which you would not
　　recognize, which you would not—how

　　　　could you? how could you?—seize.

# Impetus

In your arms, bulbs of tomatoes:
hard, half-formed. Cold ascends,
reaching the stalks first, sending
them ground-burns. The corn
dried from the inside. I once stole
ears, still in the field as the field
turned sour, struck with frost,
and no gift: dry teeth, dust sacs,
feed for the animals in winter.
Hours before ice, you pull everything
off its ropes, heirlooms hitting
the plastic bucket. Life starts
from the inside, bitter, compact,
and blooms as it softens, flushes
with age. The tomatoes might pink
if we wrapped them in paper—
as in April, the cherries we knew
by the birds that gathered and struck
before my mouth could form
the *W* want, black birds stripping
the trees, coring the sweet valves
peck by peck. Each year
we have reason to take some part
away. I hurried to bring it inside
to the table. Didn't I deserve that, one
lobed fruit, to split, to swallow, myself?

# Letter after Dismemberment

Lover, I left you because you would not slip me
    into the squares of an ice tray,

        though I asked. I was considering a jar

of preserved lemons and watching television,
    though not really, and you wondered, aloud,

        if anyone had died on camera, by accident,

if that had been captured. Want flickered in me,
    and fell, as though from a great height.

        But it must have been earlier when it came

to me: seeing the neighbor man, perhaps.
    Our tenement windows cut into him like grids,

        exposing an arm, a finger. Such mystery,

the divided flesh, like a photograph spreading
    onto a page—the body so piecemeal. Or the closet,

        being punished in the dark of overcoats

and shoes. I drew my knees to my body.
    I became a smaller box, and when your arms

        first wrapped around me, later, in love,

what could I want to give you—to give any man—
    but the tightest hold? To keep you secret

        as a stone? Then I wanted to be the stone.

I found a man, one who wanted the body in inches,
who dreamed in pixel, became divisible.

Have you hoped for anything enough to die?

Honestly, I do not remember. Not even that first
gutter of warmth when I saw the knife,

not even the last, now that I am everywhere,

in earth and in ash, in the stomach
of the one who swallowed me. And then,

when they killed him, sent him into the air

in a chambered cloud, the flies that erupted
from his belly, spun with blood, the grass,

the goats, the milk they gave. And somewhere,

I am in a girl, lightly fingering her wrists, how
her hands fit around them, thumb to index,

the pressure on the vein, the world encircled,

trapped there, the pleasure rising, and wanting
to ask for it. Then asking.

## Perrault's Tale

In the story I tell you there are two girls,

    sisters. One is beautiful, the other
    sweeps the brown cinders

over the hot bricks. It is she,

    the plainer, who meets the woman
    in the woods, who is blessed

with rose hips and juniper under

    her step, smooth stones fallen
    like words, rounded by breath.

This is how she learns to sing.

    Her sister speaks, and her tongue forks
    into snakes, leading away.

I am the woman in the woods.

    Two nights after the night I learned
    to separate sex from pain, the old

threads restitched themselves.

    He cupped his hands. I looked inside
    and saw the blue of our little world,

the drop-stitch of stars, the black jag

    where the needle had missed. We slept. I tried
    to slip my hand inside, but his fingers

were laced. My hem crept down, covering knees.

On my tongue: an amethyst, swallowed.
I don't know how to tell you

what she grew into. She was plain,

after all. The tacks were rough.
The red petals bruised under feet,

and made the kitchen floorboards

slick with blood. Her sister's snakes
scared the village away. Eventually,

the men stopped coming to the door

with axes tipped behind their heads.
The sky grew large past the half

moon of their blades. From the box

in the attic, she took the old dress.
She would let the dress out.

She would fill it with her body.

# After the Party

Sugar dries on paper plates. The cake's
decimated and barely touched. What to do
with the balloons? A few float listlessly,
unattached, still bearing like bandages
the tape that bore them to the wall.
They've gone dull, rubber tips darkening
to a bottle's pinch. It's too late, or too early.
There are too many on the floor, stirred up
as I stir. In the end, I cut them, urge a blade
into the inch between knot and blossom.
Slow deflation. It reveals what they are:
sacs of plastic, stale with air. I've seen this
before, in the newspaper picture of Nefertiti,
bound in the antechamber of a tomb,
cast out of favor—her body, barely wrapped.
How they know her: by the queenly jaw,
age of limbs and teeth. Also, by the broken
mouth, smashed by priests so she cannot
eat, cannot breathe, will never tell in the afterlife.

III

# Rabbit of the World

All our meaningful speech would not heat
a cup of water. And I have already failed.
At the end of our lives these words
will mean nothing—only if you read,
and remember the call of my skin,
how I willed you. I have seen on the pay
road, motorists turn, those who stop
for nothing slow at the sight of a hill:
Somerset County, the wind farm where
blades arch as the body, steady the air, spin
it to sparks. Imagine what it is like for me
to want you, to wait. Harbinger, rabbit
of the world, red eye flashing as if to warn:
the power that is coming will make no sound.

# The Land

When the satellite pictures
   came of the black crust,

      we knew we were alone,

and that our faults had saved us.
   This is how Venus lived:

      boiling, sealed, the surface

collapsed into the interior,
   cooled, began again.

      You walked with your new

love on Oak Island. The earth
   was descending into water,

      mined with the hollows

of treasure seekers.
   Digging ruined the soil,

      turned it up, black and gleaming,

empty on every shovel tongue.
   You searched for nothing;

      you swore you heard ghosts.

I could tell you what I know,
   the theory of a trapped past,

      as if a haunting was only

time stuck, time repeating.
    Out of our reach, Venus quiets

        for a cycle. They say dying.

I think waiting. I look at her,
    the one you have found,

        and I learn nothing about myself

except: I was not enough.
    Gorged, the land we stand upon

        is sinking. All the ghosts,

like us, are running back.

# The Ripper's Bride

Since a woman, I washed blood
from whites. What was a little

more, even if not my own? Love
is balance, a sacrifice of placement:

modulation, the way he said our eldest
died, half-born, to make room.

Others have not yet come,
but will, faces fat like suns. The way

my mother hushed: half of you is lost,
but half you will keep close like cloth.

Scrubbing married stains. They dried
like lunar phases, my hands

blanching in the cool water. You think
it wasn't possible for him to love?

Everyone loves, knows what to do,
does not question what love is.

Instead they say, under his blade
in the dark ways, the women made

no sound. Of course not. How
could they know, like me, they

were being asked for the answer?

# Salt

*A woman of twenty-six, while in prison awaiting*
*trial, succeed[ed] in committing suicide by intro-*
*ducing about 30 pins and needles in the chest*
*region, over the heart. Her method was to gently*
*introduce them, and then to press them deeper with*
*a prayer-book.*

—*Anomalies and Curiosities of Medicine, 1896*

You were the lover for which I bled. Comfort me
    with salt: tears, their silken twin. Understand

       I have made my arms doors for you. Listen:

in the quiet cell she was left with only women's
    tools—fat pincushion, muslin, thirty silver

       jabs to sew a dull square. She begged

for the Bible, knowing the temper of the hand.
    Even the openings I gave myself betrayed.

       They scabbed overnight, star clots. She drove

the points deep with the word, veined leather
    as black as her secret down. All the while

       I tasted you. But how could I contain you?

There was no slick color until the third or fourth jag
    had made its tunnel in. By then it was sure;

       her sampler would be skin. I learned

two cuts make a cross, five is a marker, then the whole
opens up to be forested: her breast before mapped

with seams, blood latitude down. I gave

everything of my body. I thought it was punishment
she wanted to escape, guilty, the dry rope waiting.

It was punishment she wanted. But I have your salt

to comfort me. Now the stars breaking through
the body bared. Now the blood, tender like touch,

flint to the tongue—and to the mouth, sweet.

## Your Marriage

On the table where I take
my meals, there is a bowl
of stones blue as teeth.
One is cleaved exactly though
I cannot find its other half,
river-smooth, white-struck—
a pestle, or hatchet's perfect
head. I can make up the story:
two fields needed a divider.
It was granite, wedged with
wood and hammer, a wall left
to winter. Cold contracts—
the plank floor, door frame,
even the mineral heart.
You must have known this;
you returned to her. I am not
a woman of substance. I look
back and you lie there, naked,
the city in ruins. My body
dissolved like grains.

# The Interpreter Tries to Blend In

It's hard in this town to find meaning
beyond what's present, what's blatant.

The churches take over theatres. Restaurants
are reborn in worship. The party stores

sell cold, single bottles. Who can blame
the students who wander, find themselves

drifting in class to the interpreter? Finger bee,
it is so like singing. It is also like rocking

life in her arms—her words, not words, not
of this world. We who are born into bright

sound breaking, don't we want what has been
denied? The store owner waits for the message,

the order from the deaf group who gather
weekly to debate over pizza. It's hard to get

anyone's attention, so he keeps coming back
to their table with pencil to point at the menu.

They are patient. The only sound is accidental,
guttural, a cry. Sometimes there's nobody

in there but them, their fingers, flying like
insects, alive at the wrists. On those nights,

he sits alert at the counter, grease on his hands,
trying not to look out.

# Nothing Happened

If I promise not to want anything,
    will you explain our accident?

        I wanted to write you a letter

on the train but I missed the train.
    In the cold I thought of this poem,

        the cold and not just the cold.

Before I knew you, in Bristol,
    a stranger's hand was bold enough

        to touch my gloved finger, test

beneath the knuckle where a wedding
    ring might sit, bulging wool. Either

        I was careful not to speak, or else

I gave myself away. Either it was
    snowing, or it was not, and you

        were away somewhere, seeing

a film, breathing in the blue light
    of strangers. Leaving a lover, once

        I said: think of all the ones you have not

yet met who will love you—
    as if, even then, they were struck

        with the knowledge of what waits,

always seeing themselves in shop
    windows, reflections spoiled by passersby.

    I knew then, or thought I knew,

what it would mean to touch you.
    But then our taxi was hit from behind.

    We were fine in the little lie moon,

fine in the backseat, behind which flickered
    glass. Nothing happened. Or else

    I saw you for what you were.

# Bug

They show no signs of finding the food,
though I've left it for weeks, though
the winter is rough and a trail of hulls
extends through the garden, and the birds,
which are said to be harbingers of things,
eat from the neighbors. In the yard: black
seeds. Holes in the telephone mouth piece.
Each one listens and sucks in speech,
gives to me voice, the ghost of a voice.
In the morning, the suction-cupped feeder's
slid from the window and splayed untouched
sunflower, hard as words from your mouth.
And now it is a dead mouth, and I think
the soul must be the voice, that which leaves
the body, that which I forgot first: music
ribbon, melody hill. In movies, the detectives
take the phone apart and find miles of curling
wire. The listening device, that sharp-tongued
piece, the bug, the plant, looks always out
of place, is pinched between finger and thumb, held
up to light. Then, *silence*! Silence. No one speaks.

# Stepmother

Save the dreams for therapy, the therapist

    said. But this dream has a train. That's new.
      And outside the window: a boy and a man

in medium coats, the boy's hood peaked

    like a dumpling—something thrown off.
      They are staring at a brick wall painted blue,

milk-blue, milk-rich, mother's cottage. No

    mother. A barn door color, a topaz earring
      stuck in a cushion. *See boy*, the man says.

*Something lost.* Hard to love, the left ones.

    Hard to fill the bent sheet, the table skirt.
      On the dresser, makeup congeals in a bottle.

Left makeup. Left shower cap. Left eyelash

    on the boy's nicked chin. The boy has left
      his lunchbox at the mother's house again. No

Tupperware returns from the mother's house,

    no shoes. No boy in the father's house now.
      No sound of boy. Not his day, which are

Sundays, Mondays, alternate Thursdays.

    In the dream, they have their backs to the train.
      In the dream, they don't even hear

the movement: passenger rattle, track breath.

The comforter had cornflowers. Let me
        fill the house with flowers, different flowers—

celery, moss—different-smelling, dusky, wood.

Let me make them turn by presence, will
        of shoulders, wind of hand. And when they do,

what light unfolding. In this part of the dream,

everything becomes blinding, a wash of what's
        after. Don't tell. But what to tell? What to interpret?

What could it mean—the boy and man turning,

their faces blurred? Even the wall goes hazy,
        unmoored. What else could it mean but I will?

**IV**

# Canary

Weather has turned the world. Ask me
where the frogs have gone. I know
the birds still standing in fields, folded
like propellers, perplexed by snow.
What was south? That was years ago,
the dream of a winged mother. It just
takes a generation, one who doesn't rise.
And then none do. Drifts fill around
them, potted in. It's not so bad, seventies
in March, coats off, daffodils opening
in a white blaze. But the polar bears
drowned, swam too far to look
for food. The ice floes lost their edges;
each shore sunk further out. Frogs,
the first barometers, on some banks
burst, blood churned with poison.
My canary shutters against the man I thought
I knew, the one who promised to love me.
What I want is a stranger's arms. What
I want is no story, the blank between
the bar and the hotel door, a snow of sheets.
Before he runs a hand over his face,
salt-struck, and explains his complications:
a child, a life. Before we have to find
our shoes. Before he knows my name,
no history, no apology, when I can trust
him, when my body blows up in his mouth.

# The Ladder Tree

The landscape turned against us.

    Earth became grass.
       The river went to rocks then returned

as a thousand small frogs. The road

    was swept under weeds, remembered
       first by animals. What love sent us

into the trees? The six young sycamores,

    we wove into a nest. Others, the locals
       dubbed circus trees, heart-shaped, hollow-

bellied. You carried always a knife. I,

    the strings for lashing. California.
       The bean and alfalfa fields. What held us?

How swiftly the saplings gave, or how long

    they bowed before breaking? Supple
       bark. Ash is softest, birch prone to bruising.

Loquat, apple. The lissome aspen, bound

    to the body of an elder—only in this way
       would the flesh accept another. Our proof:

a roadside attraction. An architect for years

    crawled under wire to water what the field
       forgot. And we forgot.

Asphalt claimed the trees. Some were split

    open, their insides tiny wires, fibrous,
        still a mystery how we got them to live.

Remember, at the hill's crown, the Ladder

    Tree, mute, rising to air? Its nine rungs,
        pruned from a pair of box elders, ending into

nothing, only sky. The other trees, the ones

    we reached, the ones we wanted to study
        or sap, were simply cut, felled by storms,

disease, insects so small as to slip beneath

    bark and eat from the inside. Love,
        stay long enough. Something will change.

# White Asparagus

How could I not imagine a difference?
For one, there was no pain. For another,
no fear. Now, bending to choose,
I choose the white asparagus for its give,
for its beauty, ghostly in the garish store,
upright in a teacup of water. I check
the ends for splits or slime. I trust it
to know where it is tender, and snap
the stalks. I know these things. I know
this chest, its network of ends, but in
the morning, the broken strands
are blonde in my fingers, whorled
with white. Whatever happened
to that old shot in which I lifted up
my shirt? It was burned or left
somewhere, or it waits in a dark place.
To get the pale shade, farmers pile
earth over the shoots, refusing them
sun, sealing the stems. We waited
for light to ripen my face as you held
the Polaroid, shook it to bring out
tan, deepen the cobalt of jeans. Color
spread up. Child, I shed my sweetness
the moment you unearthed me.
We waited in a dark of our own.

# Phlox

The funnel dropped my tree house,

    a perfect imitation of my family's
    white saltbox, on the carport.

Mother stepping on the dollhouse:

    an accident, the sitting room
    slicing her heel to the bone.

Blood on the baby wallpaper, maple

    armoire in her toes. I thought
    to trim the cowslip from shingles,

invite the splinters with a watch word,

    curl on the pitch and ruptured pine.
    My tree, I set to sweeping, slept

outside amid the cicely. I was listening

    for the odd wild, how elephants escape
    before earthquakes, white snakes

stream out of the ground. I would learn

    that kind of warn. If you do not mind
    I climbed into the wreckage.

If you do not mind I set the stump

    for dolls and tea. I was a child; I thought
    the acorn steeping in the china

was an acorn, and no fence rattle,

    train moan, butterfly blown backward
    in wind-spur would warn me

otherwise. Nor a cloud like a chiffon

    sleeve. Wait for me. Let me learn to read
    the leaves, hold the water under tongue

and sift the future. I was born inside

    your flower. If the earth says to move,
    let me swim to you through miles.

# Clean

If a mother phoned about the boys her daughter
ran with, if a brush threaded more than a loom
of pale strands, if a finger brought to the brow

a bubble of blood, the principal carded our hair,
two wooden tongue depressors borrowed

from the nurse so his fingers wouldn't touch.
Our heads bent before him in the quiet hall. He lifted
the light-catching webs, riving a white row.

Down the line the language of his hands spread,
and the mark of the dirty child was the switch.

The boy who loved me first expected the bright
blood. When he left I waited for color
to spread across the white stick, the red line

signifying my plurality. I counted time
with my tongue, naked from the waist, raw light

reflecting my bared knees like spools of silk—
the blank circle, glaring, negative. I bowed my head
for the rasp against my scalp, face rushed

with blood. *Clean*, he said. *Move on*.

## Love Letter

Hours from trees, you love my leftovers.
Beware, he will cleave like a leak.
He will stay hard only as long as you cry.
He will take himself from buttons.
He will bother you for bass. He wants
to show you the aisles he has beaten
with sighs. He wants to tell you,
*I never meant to.* In drought, the grass
cackles like crows. Much of what
you mistake for wild carrot is hemlock,
that same wedded head. The ruts
are full of fawning. The earth is clay
and cracks. There is a want from which
you cannot right yourself, a kind
of mouth which unmakes you,
robs your *no*; the way, in the heat,
you lie to yourself, say you are fine,
forget the wave until it finds you,
wrecks you, wastes you, woman
on the sidewalk: you are blood-slack,
heaving. He will leave you flat.

# The Red Thread

Pennies, chocolates wrapped in foil.

For this, each house has emptied into cars,
and the cars half-emptied while the men

look for parking, and the women, small children

attached like pockets, cross the street.
Everyone wants her child to win.

It must be about how far they swam, tails

like the turn of a fish hook, fighting
the blood in the body of the mother.

How the women too stood up quickly afterward,

sweeping off the curious hairs, and peed,
and washed, because they heard it did

something, was better than drugs or taking in Coke.

I watched you swim then sink in the shower drain.
Some part of you lingered, caught. It looked

enough like a thread that I left it. Say something, say

something about this thread. Something like:
the vein from a leaf has blown in our wake.

A red snake coils at the bottom of the drain: our child,

phrased like a question. The plum tree in back
ruptured in blight. Still, I could say nothing.

Some father is holding his girl up now so she seems

    to be at the top of the crowd, all fathers
    and daughters, Easter baskets and hands

pushing against the park place fence as if that will make it

    open faster. The links of the fence are silver
    and shaped. Her coat is pink, puffy as a bruise.

Winter has not touched her. Or rather, it has,

    in her braids and in her boots, in the way she
    scans and scans and seems to see everything

# Real Estate

Door against the white world: the realtor's
shot as seen through snow. It is called
*The Love House* because it was built

as a wedding gift. And we will probably
never see it. Nor the book barn. Nor
the one with the pink grove, blossoming

trees I should know the name of. Tulle tree?
Champagne tree? We sleep on the floor.
Then, on a pine bed. Then, when that breaks,

on the floor again. I see my thumbprints
on the lines of your cheeks. I go to death
hemmed by paper. I dream of an envelope

pressed against teeth. When I wake, it's only
the scent of you, a white hug filling my mouth,
a wish for you. Fountain tree? Shortcake

tree? Alabama tree? You don't have a desk.
I don't have a closet. We live by a favor,
called in. We live in the in-between,

and I worry we won't find them, the Italy
pictures, the sweet moon. But one shot
I remember: lying back against the boat,

my skirt flicked up to reveal my stockings,
arms around my back. We were surprised
at how low we drifted, bobbing and heaved.

We slipped under the bridges. And I knew
then, we knew: we can go anywhere. We can

float and float. We can live in the in-between.

We can live. Gondola tree. Married tree.
This is how our love came back: it never left.

## Scissors, Hammer, Hoof Pick, Awl

When the woman threatened the son of my husband,
I went to the bank. I took out all that I had
in cash. With cash, I bought coffee, croissant,
tea. With cash, I bought sugar cubes, cinnamon,
cream. I bought cheese. I bought pencils.
I bought hammocks. I bought land. I had heard
about music. I bought music. I had heard about
telescopes. I bought five. I had heard that iron
under a bed stops a nightmare. I bought scissors,
hammer, hoof pick, awl. The moon was a shoulder
blade over my shoulder. A starling buzzed us
and lifted my hair. I bought salt for cooking, salt
for bathing, salt for sleeping, salt to wake. I passed
over bills, dirty as hands. Passed through the mail-
mouth, there was a letter. In the morning, there
were threats in the snow. So I bought a poodle.
I bought a pashmina. I bought a locksmith's hour
to alter the locks. I bought a train, eighteen wheels
and a wooden engine—and I paid for it all with paper.
And the son who was six began to sing a whistling
tea kettle, telephone song. On every bill before
spending, I wrote down her phone number.
And, broke, we went home together in the dark.

# Hadrian's Wall

The pool, we built together, or rather,
    watched the earth move. A red mount

        rose as the hole was dug and emptied.

The neighbor children climbed and slid.
    We let them. And we were lazy. We dug

        already-eaten earth, a basement cave;

the pool floor kept collapsing into a gap
    beneath where roots hid, clung and cursed.

        I drew out stones like giant teeth. In Rome,

work started in the east on a stone wall,
    a rock vein, running clear to the River

        Irthing. West, the wall was sod at first,

a hair ridge, a sign. Later, slaves built
    strongholds every Roman mile to seal

        its ends, to draw a line. How could we

know this space for what it was—a cellar,
    hum of mud and fruit? The stones piled

        for our garden walls. Our water came

from an unknown place. Hadrian wept
    to watch his lover Antinous drown,

        would not be moved from Egypt. The gods

lure the ones they want from water.
    You would only wade so far, till cold or

        wetness reached your knees—I don't know

which one it was. These nights I dream
    of underneath. You're seasonal; you're staying

        only to collect your things. This wall that we

will never see—I will wait for you.
    I will wait for you there.

# Notes

"Wife" is for my husband, Jordan.

"Velata" is a portrait of a woman long believed to be Raphael's mistress. However, cleaning of the painting several years ago revealed a gold ring on her finger. There is now speculation that the painter and his subject were secretly married.

"Salt" takes as its epigraph a note from *Anomalies and Curiosities of Medicine* by Dr. George M. Gould and Dr. Walter L. Pyle, first published in 1896 by Julian Press, Inc.

"The Ladder Tree" tells the story of Axel Erlandson and his roadside attraction, the Tree Circus.

"Clean" is for my friend Allison Armbrister.

# The Brittingham Prize in Poetry
## Ronald Wallace, General Editor

*Places/Everyone* | Jim Daniels
C. K. Williams, Judge, 1985

*Talking to Strangers* | Patricia Dobler
Maxine Kumin, Judge, 1986

*Saving the Young Men of Vienna* | David Kirby
Mona Van Duyn, Judge, 1987

*Pocket Sundial* | Lisa Zeidner
Charles Wright, Judge, 1988

*Slow Joy* | Stephanie Marlis
Gerald Stern, Judge, 1989

*Level Green* | Judith Vollmer
Mary Oliver, Judge, 1990

*Salt* | Renée Ashley
Donald Finkel, Judge, 1991

*Sweet Ruin* | Tony Hoagland
Donald Justice, Judge 1992

*The Red Virgin: A Poem of Simone Weil* | Stephanie Strickland
Lisel Mueller, Judge, 1993

*The Unbeliever* | Lisa Lewis
Henry Taylor, Judge, 1994

*Old and New Testaments* | Lynn Powell
Carolyn Kizer, Judge, 1995

*Brief Landing on the Earth's Surface* | Juanita Brunk
Philip Levine, Judge, 1996

*And Her Soul Out of Nothing* | Olena Kalytiak Davis
Rita Dove, Judge, 1997

*Bardo* | Suzanne Paola
Donald Hall, Judge, 1998

*A Field Guide to the Heavens* | Frank X. Gaspar
Robert Bly, Judge, 1999

*A Path between Houses* | Greg Rappleye
Alicia Ostriker, Judge, 2000